Beyond Stocks: Exploring the World of Options.

Copyright @ Svetla Genova.

Author : Svetla Genova.

Table of content

Introduction

Are you intrigued by the world of finance and want to explore an exciting way to invest and make money? This book is designed specifically for beginners, who are eager to embark on a journey of financial discovery. We will break down the complexities of options trading and present them in an accessible and easy-to-understand manner. You'll gain a clear and comprehensive understanding of what options are, how they work, and how to use them to your advantage.

Who Is This Book For?

Complete Novices: If you've never invested before and find the financial jargon and complexity of investing overwhelming, this book is tailored to your needs. We break down the basics in a clear manner, ensuring you feel comfortable taking your first steps in the world of investments.

Young Adults and Students: If you're a young adult or a student looking to kickstart your financial future, this book provides essential information on how to begin building wealth early. Learn how to make your money work for you, even with limited resources.

Parents and Guardians: Teach your children the value of financial literacy and investing with this book.

Savers Looking to Grow Their Wealth: If you've been saving money in a regular savings account and want to explore better ways to grow your wealth, this book will introduce you to various investment options that can potentially offer higher returns.

Income Seekers: Are you looking for ways to generate additional income from your investments? Options can provide strategies for income generation, and this book explores those techniques.

Diversification Enthusiasts: If you believe in diversifying your investments to reduce risk, this book will demonstrate how options can be a valuable addition to your diversified portfolio.

Curious Learners: Even if you have a basic understanding of stocks and investing, but you're curious about options and want to explore this fascinating world further, this book will be your comprehensive guide.

Chapter 1

What are options?

Options trading can seem like a daunting venture, especially for those who are new to the financial markets. The terminology alone can be enough to make your head spin: calls, puts, premiums, spreads, straddles, and leaps - it all sounds rather complex. However, fear not, for in this book, we aim to simplify the world of options and make it accessible to anyone who is curious and eager to learn. So, welcome to the world of options, where we will take you on a journey from the very basics to more advanced strategies, all explained in the simplest way possible.

The Basics of Options

Let's start at the beginning: what are the options? At their core, options are financial instruments that give you the right, but not the obligation, to buy or sell an underlying asset at a specific price on or before a predetermined expiration date. This underlying asset can be just about anything, but in the context of our discussion, we'll focus on options tied to stocks.

Imagine you're in the market for a new car, and you find your dream car at a dealership. The dealer tells you that you can reserve the car for a small fee, but you don't have to buy it if you change your mind. This reservation fee is like the premium you pay when buying an option. If you decide not to buy the car, you lose the fee, but you're not obligated to make the purchase.

Options come in two primary flavors: call options and put options.

Call Options

A call option is like a financial contract that gives you the right to buy a specific number of shares of a particular stock at a predetermined price, known as the strike price, before a specified expiration date. Think of it as making a reservation to buy stock at a certain price.

For example, suppose you believe that XYZ Company's stock, currently trading at $50 per share, will rise in value in the next few months. You could purchase a call option with a strike price of $55 for a premium of $3. This means that, by paying $3, you secure the right to buy XYZ Company's stock at $55 per share before the option's expiration date.

If, by the time the option expires, the stock's price has risen to $60 per share, you can exercise your call option and buy the stock for $55, even though it's now trading at $60. You've just made a $5 profit per share ($60 - $55), minus the $3 premium you initially paid for the option. In total, you've made a $2 profit per share ($5 - $3).

Put Options

On the flip side, put options give you the right to sell a specific number of shares of a particular stock at a predetermined price before a specified expiration date. Put options are like insurance policies against falling stock prices.

For instance, let's say you own 100 shares of ABC Corporation, currently trading at $70 per share. Worried that the stock's price might drop in the next few months, you purchase a put option with a strike price of $65 for a premium of $2. This means you have the right to sell your shares for $65 each, no matter what the market price is, before the option expires.

If, by the time the option expires, the stock's price falls to $60 per share, you can exercise your put option and sell your shares for $65 each, even though they are only worth $60 on the market. This protects you from the $5-per-share loss ($65 - $60), minus the $2 premium you paid for the option. In total, you've limited your loss to $3 per share ($5 - $2).

The Power of Options

Options offer a unique flexibility that makes them a valuable tool for investors and traders. Here are some key advantages:

- ❖ Limited Risk: When you buy an option, the most you can lose is the premium you paid for it. This limited risk makes options an attractive choice for risk-averse investors.

- ❖ Leverage: Options allow you to control a larger position in the underlying asset with a relatively small investment. This leverage can amplify your gains if the market moves in your favor.

❖ Income Generation: Options can be used to generate income. For example, selling covered call options on stocks you already own can provide regular income in the form of premiums.

❖ Risk Management: Put options can act as insurance against declining asset prices. They provide a way to limit your losses in a bearish market.

❖ Diversification: Options can be used to diversify your portfolio and tailor your risk exposure to your financial goals.

Navigating Bullish and Bearish Markets

Before we dive deeper into the world of options strategies, it's crucial to understand market sentiment, as it plays a significant role in your trading decisions. Markets can generally be categorized as bullish or bearish:

Bullish Market: In a bullish market, investors are optimistic, and stock prices tend to rise. Positive economic indicators, strong corporate earnings, or other favorable news can drive bullish sentiment.

Bearish Market: In contrast, a bearish market is characterized by pessimism and falling stock prices. Negative economic news, poor corporate earnings, or other adverse events can trigger bearish sentiment.

Your outlook on the market can influence your options trading strategy. In a bullish market, you might lean toward call options, aiming to profit from rising stock prices. In a bearish market, put options can help protect your portfolio from potential losses.

Understanding market sentiment is the first step in making informed decisions about which options strategies to employ. We'll explore these strategies in detail in the upcoming chapters, ensuring you have the knowledge and confidence to navigate both bullish and bearish markets effectively.

Buying and selling stock vs. options

Buying and selling stocks and options are two common ways to invest in the financial markets, each with its own characteristics, risks, and potential rewards. Let's explore these two investment strategies in more detail:

Buying and Selling Stocks:

1. Ownership:

When you buy a stock, you are purchasing a share of ownership in a company.

As a shareholder, you have certain rights, such as voting in shareholder meetings and receiving dividends (if the company pays them).

2. Potential for Growth:

Stocks can appreciate in value over time, potentially offering long-term capital appreciation.

Stockholders benefit from a company's success as its stock price rises.

3. Income Generation:

Some stocks pay dividends, providing a steady stream of income to shareholders.

Investors can choose dividend stocks for regular income in addition to potential capital gains.

4. Risks:

Stock prices can be volatile, leading to potential losses if the market declines.

There's no limit to the potential loss when owning stocks; a stock's value can go to zero.

5. Investment Timeframe:

Stock investing is typically considered a longer-term strategy, although short-term trading is also common.

Buying and Selling Options:

1. Derivative Contracts:

Options are derivative contracts that give you the right, but not the obligation, to buy (call option) or sell (put option) a specific number of shares at a predetermined price (strike price) by a certain expiration date.

2. Leverage:

Options provide leverage, allowing you to control a larger position with a smaller investment.

This leverage can amplify both gains and losses, making options riskier than stocks.

3. Flexibility:

Options can be used for various strategies, including hedging, income generation, and speculation.

Traders can employ options to customize their risk-reward profile to a greater extent than with stocks alone.

4. Limited Loss Potential:

When buying options, your maximum loss is limited to the premium you paid for the option contract.

This limited downside can be appealing, especially for risk management.

5. Expiration Date:

Options have expiration dates, which means they have a finite lifespan.

Shorter-term trading is more common in the options market.

6. Complexity:

Options can be complex and may require a deeper understanding of market dynamics and strategies.

It's essential to educate yourself before trading options to avoid unexpected losses.

7. Risk Management:

Options can be used as a risk management tool, allowing investors to protect their stock portfolios from adverse price movements.

8. Speculation:

Some traders use options for speculative purposes, aiming to profit from price movements in the underlying stock without owning the stock itself.

9. Margin Requirements:

If you write (sell) options, you may need to post collateral or margin to cover potential losses, which can tie up capital.

In summary, buying and selling stocks represents ownership in a company, offering potential for long-term growth and income but with unlimited loss potential. On the other hand, trading options involves derivative contracts with leverage, flexibility, and defined risk, making them suitable for various strategies but also more complex and potentially riskier. The choice between stocks and options depends on your investment goals, risk tolerance, and understanding of the financial markets. Many investors use both stocks and options within a diversified portfolio to achieve their financial objectives while managing risk.

Welcome to the exciting world of options! We've just scratched the surface of what options are and how they can be used to your advantage. Throughout this book, we'll guide you through various options strategies, from the straightforward to the more advanced, all explained in the simplest way possible.

Whether you're a novice investor looking to dip your toes into options trading or someone with some experience seeking to expand your knowledge, we're here to help you build a strong foundation and enhance your understanding of this intriguing financial instrument. Remember, options trading, like any investment activity, requires practice and patience. So, let's embark on this journey together and demystify the world of options.

Chapter 2

Bullish and Bearish Markets

The world of finance is a complex and dynamic one, driven by a multitude of factors that influence market behavior. Two fundamental and opposing sentiments that shape the financial landscape are bullish and bearish markets. Understanding these sentiments is crucial for investors, as they play a pivotal role in shaping investment strategies and decisions. In this article, we will delve into the concepts of bullish and bearish markets, exploring their characteristics, causes, and the profound impact they have on investment decisions.

The Bullish Market: Optimism Rules

A bullish market, often referred to as a bull market, is characterized by a prevailing sense of optimism among investors. During such periods, the prices of financial assets, such as stocks, bonds, and commodities, tend to rise over an extended period. Several key characteristics define a bullish market:

> ➤ Rising Asset Prices: The primary hallmark of a bullish market is the consistent upward movement of asset prices. This increase in prices is driven by a higher demand for assets, often fueled by positive economic indicators, strong corporate earnings, and favorable government policies.

➤ Investor Confidence: Bull markets are marked by a high level of investor confidence. Investors believe that the good times will continue, and they are more willing to take on risks in pursuit of potentially higher returns. This increased risk appetite can lead to increased trading activity and liquidity in the market.

➤ Strong Economic Fundamentals: A bullish market is typically associated with a strong and growing economy. Low unemployment rates, robust GDP growth, and increasing consumer spending are common indicators of a bullish economic backdrop.

➤ Buoyant Sentiment: Positive news and sentiment prevail in a bull market. Media headlines often highlight the successes of investors who have profited handsomely from their investments, reinforcing the positive sentiment.

➤ Favorable Monetary Policy: Central banks may implement accommodative monetary policies, such as lowering interest rates or engaging in quantitative easing, to support economic growth during a bull market. These policies can further boost investor confidence and asset prices.

➤ Long-Term Growth: Bull markets are often associated with long-term investment strategies. Investors are more likely to buy and hold assets, anticipating that they will continue to appreciate in value over time.

The Bearish Market: Pessimism Takes Hold

Conversely, a bearish market, or bear market, is characterized by pessimism and a sustained decline in asset prices. Investors in a bear market are generally cautious and risk-averse, leading to the following defining features:

➢ Falling Asset Prices: The most prominent feature of a bear market is a consistent decline in the prices of financial assets. This decline is usually driven by factors such as economic downturns, poor corporate earnings, or adverse geopolitical events.

➢ Low Investor Confidence: In a bear market, investor confidence is low. Investors are concerned about the future performance of their investments and may choose to sell assets to minimize potential losses. This can lead to increased selling pressure and lower liquidity in the market.

➢ Economic Challenges: Bear markets are often accompanied by economic challenges, including rising unemployment, stagnant or contracting GDP, and reduced consumer spending. These economic headwinds can contribute to the negative sentiment in the market.

➢ Negative Sentiment: Media headlines during bear markets tend to focus on losses and economic difficulties. Stories of investors losing significant amounts of money can intensify the prevailing negative sentiment.

➢ Tightened Monetary Policy: Central banks may respond to economic challenges by implementing restrictive monetary policies, such as raising interest rates. While these policies are designed to curb inflation and stabilize the economy, they can further exacerbate the bearish sentiment in financial markets.

➢ Short-Term Trading: Bear markets often see increased short-term trading as investors attempt to profit from declining prices. This heightened trading activity can lead to higher market volatility.

How Market Sentiment Impacts Your Decisions

Understanding market sentiment, whether bullish or bearish, is essential for investors as it profoundly influences their decision-making processes. Here's how market sentiment impacts investment decisions:

❖ Asset Allocation: Market sentiment plays a crucial role in determining asset allocation within an investment portfolio. In a bullish market, investors may allocate a higher proportion of their portfolio to equities, seeking higher returns.

Conversely, in a bearish market, they may shift towards safer assets like bonds or cash to preserve capital.

❖ Risk Tolerance: Market sentiment affects an investor's risk tolerance. During bullish periods, investors are more willing to take on higher-risk investments, whereas bear markets may prompt a more conservative approach.

❖ Timing of Investments: Market sentiment can influence the timing of investment decisions. In a bullish market, investors may be more inclined to buy assets at higher prices, fearing that they will miss out on further gains. In contrast, during bear markets, investors may hold off on purchases, waiting for signs of a market bottom.

❖ Diversification Strategies: Bullish and bearish markets can impact diversification strategies. Bull markets may lead to an overconcentration of assets in certain sectors or industries, while bear markets may prompt investors to diversify their portfolios to reduce risk.

❖ Investment Horizon: Market sentiment can affect an investor's investment horizon. In a bullish market, investors may have a longer-term perspective, whereas the uncertainty of a bear market may lead to shorter holding periods and more frequent trading.

❖ Emotional Bias: Emotions often run high in both bullish and bearish markets. Greed and overconfidence may drive investment decisions in bull markets, while fear and panic can lead to hasty decisions in bear markets. It's essential for investors to manage their emotional biases and make rational decisions based on their financial goals and risk tolerance.

❖ Investment Strategy: Market sentiment can shape an investor's overall investment strategy. During a bull market, a "buy and hold" strategy may be more popular, while a bear market may lead to more active trading or a defensive investment approach.

❖ Risk Management: In bear markets, risk management becomes paramount. Investors may use strategies like stop-loss orders or hedging to protect their portfolios from significant losses. Risk management techniques are less commonly employed in bull markets when optimism prevails.

Bullish and bearish markets are two opposing forces that drive the financial markets. Bull markets are characterized by optimism, rising asset prices, and investor confidence, while bear markets are marked by pessimism, falling prices, and caution. Understanding these market sentiments is essential for investors, as they greatly impact investment decisions.

Investors must recognize that market sentiment is not static and can change rapidly in response to economic, political, and social events. Successful investors adapt their strategies to prevailing market conditions and maintain a long-term perspective while managing their emotions and risk.

Ultimately, whether in a bullish or bearish market, the key to successful investing lies in having a well-defined investment plan, diversifying your portfolio, and staying informed about market developments. By doing so, investors can navigate the ever-changing landscape of financial markets and work towards achieving their long-term financial goals.

Chapter 3

Call and Put Options

Options are financial instruments that provide traders and investors with a versatile toolset to manage risk and speculate on price movements in various markets. Among the most traded options are call options and put options, which allow market participants to bet on price upside or downside, respectively. In this comprehensive guide, we will delve deep into the world of call and put options, exploring their mechanics, strategies, and real-world examples.

Understanding Call Options

A call option grants the holder the right, but not the obligation, to buy a specific asset, typically a stock, at a predetermined price, known as the strike price, before or on a specified expiration date. This right comes at a cost, known as the premium, which the option buyer pays to the option seller.

Mechanics of a Call Option

Strike Price: The strike price is the price at which the option holder has the right to purchase the underlying asset. It is a crucial component of the call option contract and is set at the time of purchase.

Expiration Date: The expiration date is the date on which the call option contract expires. After this date, the option holder can no longer exercise their right to buy the underlying asset.

Premium: The premium is the price the option buyer pays to the option seller to acquire the call option. It represents the cost of holding the option and is determined by various factors, including the volatility of the underlying asset, time until expiration, and the difference between the strike price and the current market price of the asset.

Option Holder vs. Option Writer: The option holder (buyer) is the party that acquires the right to buy the underlying asset, while the option writer (seller) is the party that grants this right in exchange for the premium.

Exercise: Exercising a call option means using the right to buy the underlying asset at the strike price. This is usually done when the market price of the asset is higher than the strike price, allowing the option holder to profit from the price difference.

Real-World Example - Call Options

Suppose you are an investor interested in buying shares of XYZ Corporation, which is currently trading at $50 per share. However, you believe that the stock price will rise significantly in the next three months. To capitalize on this expected price increase while limiting your risk, you decide to purchase a call option.

You buy one XYZ Corporation call option with a strike price of $55 and a premium of $3 per share. This call option contract has a three-month expiration date. By purchasing this call option:

You have the right to buy 100 shares of XYZ Corporation at $55 per share (the strike price) within the next three months.

You pay a premium of $3 per share, which totals $300 for the entire contract.

Scenario 1: Bullish Outcome

Three months later, the stock price of XYZ Corporation has indeed risen to $60 per share. Since your call option allows you to buy shares at $55 each, you can exercise your option and buy 100 shares for a total of $5,500. However, you've already paid a $300 premium for the option, so your net cost is $5,800 ($5,500 for the shares plus $300 premium).

You can now sell your 100 shares in the open market at the current market price of $60 each, yielding $6,000 in revenue. After deducting your net cost of $5,800, you have a profit of $200.

Scenario 2: Unfavorable Outcome

If, on the other hand, the stock price of XYZ Corporation remains below $55 per share or only slightly increases, you may choose not to exercise the call option. In this case, you would lose the $300 premium paid for the option, but your potential losses are limited to that amount, and you do not need to buy the underlying shares.

Understanding Put Options

A put option, in contrast to a call option, provides the holder with the right, but not the obligation, to sell a specific asset at a predetermined strike price before or on a specified expiration date. Put options are used by investors and traders to profit from price declines in the underlying asset.

Mechanics of a Put Option

Strike Price: Like call options, the strike price is the price at which the option holder can sell the underlying asset.

Expiration Date: The expiration date is the date on which the put option contract expires. After this date, the option holder can no longer exercise their right to sell the underlying asset.

Premium: The premium is the price the option buyer pays to the option seller to acquire the put option. It reflects the cost of holding the option and is influenced by factors such as the asset's volatility and time until expiration.

Option Holder vs. Option Writer: The option holder (buyer) has the right to sell the underlying asset, while the option writer (seller) is obligated to buy the asset if the option holder decides to exercise the put option.

Exercise: Exercising a put option means using the right to sell the underlying asset at the strike price. This is typically done when the market price of the asset is lower than the strike price, allowing the option holder to profit from the price difference.

Real-World Example - Put Options

Suppose you are an investor who holds a portfolio of stocks and is concerned about a potential market downturn. You want to protect your investments from declining prices. To do this, you decide to purchase put options on some of the stocks in your portfolio.

Let's say you own 500 shares of ABC Corporation, which is currently trading at $70 per share. To hedge against a possible price drop, you buy five put options on ABC Corporation with a strike price of $65 and a premium of $2 per share. Each put option contract represents 100 shares and has a two-month expiration date.

By purchasing these put options:

You have the right to sell 500 shares of ABC Corporation at $65 per share (the strike price) within the next two months.

You pay a premium of $2 per share, totaling $1,000 for all five contracts.

Scenario 1: Bearish Outcome

During the two-month period, the stock price of ABC Corporation experiences a significant decline due to market volatility, dropping to $60 per share. Given that your put options allow you to sell your 500 shares at $65 each, you decide to exercise the options.

You sell 500 shares at $65 each, yielding $32,500 in total revenue. However, you've already paid a $1,000 premium for the put options. Subtracting the premium from your revenue, you have a net profit of $31,500. This profit offsets the losses in your stock portfolio caused by the declining market.

Scenario 2: Unfavorable Outcome

If, instead, the stock price of ABC Corporation remains stable or even increases during the two-month period, you may choose not to exercise the put options. In this case, you would lose the $1,000 premium paid for the options, but your potential losses in the stock portfolio are not magnified by the decline in share prices because you retained the right to sell at the strike price.

Strategies Involving Call and Put Options

The versatility of call and put options allows traders and investors to implement various strategies to achieve specific financial objectives. Here are some common strategies involving these options:

- ➢ Covered Call: In a covered call strategy, an investor who owns the underlying asset (e.g., stock) sells call options on that asset. This generates income from the premium received, but the investor is obligated to sell the asset at the strike price if the option is exercised.

- ➢ Protective Put: Also known as a married put, this strategy involves purchasing a put option to protect an existing stock position from potential losses. It acts as insurance against a decline in the stock's value.

- ➢ Straddle: A straddle strategy involves buying both a call option and a put option with the same strike price and expiration date. It is used when an investor anticipates a significant price movement but is uncertain about the direction (up or down).

- ➢ Strangle: Like a straddle, a strangle strategy involves buying out-of-the-money call and put options with different strike prices. It is used when an investor expects price volatility but is unsure about the direction and wants to reduce the cost of the strategy compared to a straddle.

- ➢ Long Call or Put: A simple strategy is buying either a long call or a long put option. A long call benefits from price increases, while a long put benefits from price decreases. These strategies offer limited risk (the premium paid) and potentially unlimited reward.

➤ Iron Condor: This strategy combines a bear call spread (selling a call option with a higher strike price and buying a call option with a lower strike price) with a bull put spread (selling a put option with a lower strike price and buying a put option with a higher strike price). It is used when the investor expects the underlying asset to trade within a specific range.

Real-World Example - Options Strategies

Suppose you are a trader who believes that a technology company's stock, TechCo Inc., is about to release a highly anticipated product that will create significant market volatility. You want to capitalize on this volatility but want to limit your potential losses. Here's how you could use options strategies:

➤ Straddle Strategy: You buy one call option with a strike price of $150 and a premium of $5 per share and simultaneously purchase one put option with a strike price of $150 and a premium of $5 per share. The stock is currently trading at $150.

If the stock price rises above $155 or falls below $145, you will profit from either the call or the put option.

If the stock price remains near $150, your losses are limited to the total premium paid for both options ($10 per share).

➤ Covered Call Strategy: You already own 100 shares of TechCo Inc. stock, which you bought at $140 per share. You sell one call option with a strike price of $155 for a premium of $5 per share.

➤ If the stock price remains below $155, you keep the premium and continue holding your shares.

If the stock price rises above $155, you may be obligated to sell your shares at the strike price, but you benefit from the premium received and any profit from the stock's appreciation.

➤ Protective Put Strategy: You own 200 shares of TechCo Inc. stock, which you purchased at $160 per share. You buy two put options with a strike price of $150 for a premium of $4 per share each.

➤ If the stock price falls below $150, your put options will increase in value, offsetting losses in the stock position.

➤ If the stock price remains above $150, you've limited your potential losses to the premium paid for the put options.

Risks and Considerations

While call and put options offer opportunities for profit and risk management, they are not without risks and complexities. Here are some key considerations:

➤ Limited Time: Options have expiration dates, which means they have a limited lifespan. The closer they get to expiration, the more rapidly their value can erode.

➤ Price Volatility: Options can be highly sensitive to changes in the price and volatility of the underlying asset. Higher volatility can lead to larger price swings in options, affecting their premiums.

➤ Leverage: Options provide leverage, allowing traders to control a larger position with a smaller upfront investment. While this can amplify profits, it also increases potential losses.

➤ Assignment Risk: For option writers (sellers), there is the risk of being assigned the obligation to buy or sell the underlying asset. This can happen at any time before expiration, especially if the option is in-the-money.

➤ Complexity: Options can be complex, especially when used in combination with other options or strategies. It's important for traders to thoroughly understand the strategies they are using.

➤ Cost of Trading: Frequent buying and selling of options can lead to significant transaction costs, including commissions and bid-ask spreads.

➢ Market Timing: Timing is crucial when trading options. Accurately predicting price movements within a specific timeframe is challenging.

Call and put options are powerful financial instruments that provide traders and investors with the flexibility to profit from both rising and falling markets while managing risk. Understanding their mechanics, strategies, and associated risks is essential for those looking to incorporate options into their investment toolkit.

Whether you are an individual investor seeking to protect your portfolio or a seasoned trader looking for opportunities in the market, call and put options offer a wide range of possibilities. With careful analysis, risk management, and the right strategy, options can be a valuable addition to your financial arsenal, enabling you to navigate the complex world of finance with confidence and agility.

Chapter 4

Covered Call Strategy

Introduction to the Covered Call

The covered call strategy is a popular options trading strategy that involves owning an underlying asset, such as stocks, and simultaneously selling call options on that asset. It is a relatively conservative strategy often used by investors who want to generate income from their existing stock holdings while potentially limiting their downside risk.

In a covered call strategy, two key components come into play:

Underlying Asset: The investor owns a certain amount of the underlying asset, typically shares of a stock. This is the "covered" part of the strategy because the investor holds the asset to cover the obligation of the call options.

Call Options: The investor sells call options on the same underlying asset they own. Each call option represents the right (but not the obligation) for the holder to buy the underlying asset at a specified price (strike price) on or before a specified date (expiration date).

How It Works: Writing Covered Calls

The process of implementing a covered call strategy involves the following steps:

Select the Underlying Asset: Choose a stock or another underlying asset that you already own or are willing to buy.

Choose the Call Option: Select a call option contract to sell. This includes deciding on the strike price and expiration date for the option. The strike price is the price at which the buyer of the call option can purchase the underlying asset.

Sell the Call Option: Write (or sell) the call option. By doing this, you receive a premium from the buyer of the call option. This premium is yours to keep, regardless of what happens next.

Wait and Monitor: As the option seller, you wait until the expiration date. If the stock price remains below the strike price, the call option expires worthless, and you keep the premium as profit.

Manage the Position: If the stock price rises significantly and you're concerned about losing your shares if the call option is exercised, you can choose to buy back the call option before expiration to close out the position. This can be done by buying the same call option you initially sold.

When to Use the Covered Call Strategy

The covered call strategy is typically used in the following situations:

Generate Income: Investors use covered calls to generate additional income from their stock holdings. The premium received from selling call options provides a steady cash flow.

Moderate Bullish Outlook: It's most effective when an investor has a moderately bullish outlook for the underlying asset. They believe the asset's price will rise slightly or remain relatively stable.

Reducing Downside Risk: Writing covered calls provides some downside protection since the premium received reduces the effective purchase price of the stock. However, this protection is limited to the premium received.

Stocks with Low Volatility: Covered calls are often used with stocks that have low volatility since the strategy benefits from the stable or slightly rising prices of the underlying asset.

Risks and Rewards

Rewards:

Income Generation: The primary benefit of the covered call strategy is the premium income received from selling call options. This income can enhance the overall return on the underlying asset.

Limited Downside Risk: The premium collected from selling the call option partially offsets potential losses in the underlying asset's value. This can provide a cushion during market downturns.

Retention of Stock Ownership: You maintain ownership of the underlying asset throughout the strategy, allowing you to benefit from any potential stock price appreciation.

Risks:

Capped Profit Potential: By selling a call option, you limit your potential profit from the underlying asset. If the stock price rises significantly, your gains are capped at the strike price plus the premium received.

Obligation to Sell: If the stock price rises above the strike price, the call option may be exercised, obligating you to sell your shares at the strike price. You may miss out on potential future gains if the stock continues to rise.

Market Risk: The covered call strategy does not eliminate market risk entirely. If the underlying asset's price experiences a significant decline, your losses will be partially offset by the premium received but not fully protected.

Opportunity Cost: If the stock experiences substantial price appreciation, you may regret having sold the call option because you'll miss out on potential profits above the strike price.

In conclusion, the covered call strategy is a versatile approach that provides income generation and limited downside protection for investors. It is crucial to carefully select the underlying asset, strike price, and expiration date to align with your financial goals and market outlook. Additionally, understanding the associated risks is essential to effectively manage your covered call positions.

Chapter 5

DITM Leaps

"DITM Leaps" stands for "Deep In The Money Leaps," and they are a specific type of options contract that offers unique features and advantages compared to standard options. Let's delve deeper into DITM Leaps, how they differ from standard options, and their potential benefits and considerations:

1. What Are DITM Leaps?

DITM Leaps are long-term call options or LEAPS (Long-term Equity Anticipation Securities) that are deep in the money. In the context of options, "in the money" means that the option has intrinsic value because the strike price is favorable relative to the current market price of the underlying asset. A deep in the money option is one where the intrinsic value is significantly higher than the time premium, which is the extra cost associated with the time left until the option's expiration.

For example, if you have a DITM Leap call option for a stock with a strike price of $50 when the stock is currently trading at $70, the intrinsic value of the option is $20 ($70 - $50), and the time premium may be relatively low compared to this intrinsic value because of the option's long-term nature.

2. How Leaps Differ from Standard Options

Here are some key differences between DITM Leaps and standard options:

Longer Time Horizon: DITM Leaps typically have a longer time until expiration compared to most standard options. Standard options usually expire within a few months, while DITM Leaps can have expirations of one year or more.

Higher Intrinsic Value: DITM Leaps have a higher intrinsic value relative to their premium cost compared to standard options. This intrinsic value provides a cushion against adverse price movements of the underlying asset.

Lower Time Premium: Since DITM Leaps have a longer time until expiration, the time premium (extrinsic value) is relatively lower compared to standard options with shorter expiration periods.

Lower Leverage: While DITM Leaps offer lower potential returns compared to out-of-the-money (OTM) options, they also come with lower risk due to their deep in the money status and reduced exposure to time decay.

3. Potential Benefits and Considerations

Benefits of DITM Leaps:

- Reduced Risk: DITM Leaps offer a more conservative approach to options trading because their intrinsic value provides a significant safety net against adverse price movements in the underlying asset.

- Longer Time Horizon: Investors who want to maintain exposure to an underlying asset over an extended period can benefit from DITM Leaps by avoiding the need to continuously roll over shorter-term options.

- Lower Time Decay: The reduced time premium means that DITM Leaps are less affected by time decay, making them more suitable for investors who want to hold positions for an extended period.

Considerations for DITM Leaps:

- Higher Upfront Cost: DITM Leaps typically have a higher upfront cost due to their deep intrinsic value. This can require a larger initial investment.

- Lower Potential Returns: While DITM Leaps offer reduced risk, they also offer lower potential returns compared to out-of-the-money options, which can provide substantial gains if the underlying asset makes significant price movements in the desired direction.

- Market Conditions: The suitability of DITM Leaps depends on market conditions and an investor's risk tolerance. In a highly volatile market, DITM Leaps may provide more stability, but they may underperform in bull markets when higher-risk options could yield better returns.

In summary, DITM Leaps are a specific type of options contract that provides a conservative, long-term approach to options trading. They offer reduced risk, longer time horizons, and lower exposure to time decay but come with a higher upfront cost and lower potential returns compared to standard options. The choice between DITM Leaps and standard options depends on an investor's goals, risk tolerance, and market outlook.

Chapter 6

Credit and Debit Spreads

Credit spreads are a popular options trading strategy that involves simultaneously buying and selling options contracts. This strategy is designed to generate income while limiting the trader's risk exposure. Credit spreads are also known as net credit spreads because they result in a net credit to the trader's account when initially established. In this article, we will explore credit spreads in detail, including how they work, the different types of credit spreads, and when and how to implement them.

How Credit Spreads Work

Credit spreads involve two options contracts: a short option and a long option. The short option is typically closer to the current market price, while the long option is farther away from the market price. The combination of these two options creates net credit, which is the premium received when the trade is executed.

The most common types of credit spreads are the bear call spread and the bull put spread. Let's take a closer look at each of these:

Bear Call Spread: In a bear call spread, you sell a call option with a lower strike price and simultaneously buy a call option with a higher strike price. Both options have the same expiration date. This strategy is used when you expect the underlying asset's price to decline or remain relatively flat.

Example: Suppose you believe that Company XYZ's stock, currently trading at $50, will decrease in value. You could sell a call option with a strike price of $55 (short call) and simultaneously buy a call option with a strike price of $60 (long call), both expiring in one month. You receive a net credit for this trade, which is your profit potential.

Bull Put Spread: In a bull put spread, you sell a put option with a higher strike price and simultaneously buy a put option with a lower strike price, both with the same expiration date. This strategy is used when you expect the underlying asset's price to rise or remain relatively stable.

Example: Let's say you believe that Company ABC's stock, currently trading at $75, will increase in value. You could sell a put option with a strike price of $70 (short put) and simultaneously buy a put option with a strike price of $65 (long put), both expiring in one month. Like the bear call spread, you receive net credit for this trade.

Benefits of Credit Spreads

Credit spreads offer several advantages to traders:

Income Generation: The primary goal of credit spreads is to generate income. When you establish a credit spread, you receive a premium upfront, which is yours to keep if the options expire worthless or close to it.

Limited Risk: One of the key benefits of credit spreads is that they come with limited risk. Your maximum potential loss is known at the time of trade initiation and is typically the difference between the strike prices of the options minus the net credit received.

Time Decay Advantage: Credit spreads benefit from time decay, also known as theta decay. As time passes, the options you sold lose value more rapidly than the options you bought, potentially allowing you to close the trade for a profit before expiration.

Flexibility: Credit spreads can be tailored to your market outlook. You can adjust the strike prices and expiration dates to align with your expectations for the underlying asset's price movement.

Debit Spreads: Managing Risk with Defined Costs

While credit spreads involve selling options to generate income, debit spreads are a risk management strategy that involves buying options to limit potential losses. Debit spreads are also known as net debit spreads because they result in a net debit to the trader's account when established. Let's delve into how debit spreads work, their types, and when to implement them.

How Debit Spreads Work

Debit spreads involve two options contracts, just like credit spreads, but in this case, you are buying both options. The goal of a debit spread is to reduce the cost of purchasing options while also defining the maximum potential loss. This is achieved by simultaneously buying a cheaper option (usually out-of-the-money) and selling a more expensive option (usually in-the-money).

The two common types of debit spreads are the bull call spread and the bear put spread:

Bull Call Spread: In a bull call spread, you buy a call option with a lower strike price and simultaneously sell a call option with a higher strike price. Both options have the same expiration date. This strategy is used when you expect the underlying asset's price to rise.

Example: Suppose you believe that Tech Company XYZ's stock, currently trading at $60, will go up in value. You could buy a call option with a strike price of $55 (long call) and simultaneously sell a call option with a strike price of $60 (short call), both expiring in one month. This trade will result in a net debit, which represents your maximum potential loss.

Bear Put Spread: In a bear put spread, you buy a put option with a higher strike price and simultaneously sell a put option with a lower strike price, both with the same expiration date. This strategy is used when you expect the underlying asset's price to decline.

Example: Let's say you believe that Oil Company ABC's stock, currently trading at $45, will decrease in value. You could buy a put option with a strike price of $50 (long put) and simultaneously sell a put option with a strike price of $45 (short put), both expiring in one month. This trade will also result in a net debit, representing your maximum potential loss.

Benefits of Debit Spreads

Debit spreads offer several advantages to traders, primarily centered around risk management:

Limited Risk: The primary benefit of debit spreads is that they come with limited risk. Your maximum potential loss is known at the time of trade initiation and is typically the net debit paid for the spread.

Cost Reduction: Debit spreads allow you to reduce the cost of buying options. By selling an option with a higher premium, you offset the cost of purchasing the option with a lower premium.

Defined Maximum Loss: Unlike simply buying a single option, where your loss potential is unlimited, debit spreads define your maximum potential loss, which can be a reassuring feature for risk-averse traders.

Potential for Profit: Debit spreads can also profit from favorable price movements in the underlying asset, but their primary purpose is to limit risk rather than generate income.

When and How to Implement These Strategies

The decision to implement credit or debit spreads depends on your market outlook, risk tolerance, and trading goals. Here's a guide on when and how to use these strategies effectively:

Credit Spreads:

Market Outlook: Credit spreads are best suited for neutral to mildly bearish or bullish market conditions. If you anticipate that the underlying asset will move within a certain range or remain relatively stable, credit spreads can be a viable choice.

Income Generation: Use credit spreads when your primary objective is to generate income from options premiums. The income received upfront can be used as a potential source of profit.

Risk Management: While credit spreads have limited risk compared to outright options selling, they are not risk-free. Be sure to manage risk by using appropriate position sizing and stop-loss orders.

Time Horizon: Credit spreads typically have a shorter time horizon, as you aim to capitalize on time decay. Consider shorter expiration dates when implementing this strategy.

Debit Spreads:

Market Outlook: Debit spreads are suitable when you have a clear bullish or bearish outlook on the underlying asset. If you expect a significant price movement, debit spreads can help manage risk while offering profit potential.

Risk Management: Use debit spreads when capital preservation and risk management are your top priorities. The defined maximum loss provides peace of mind in volatile markets.

Cost Efficiency: Debit spreads allow you to participate in the price movement of an underlying asset while reducing the cost of entering the trade. This can be especially useful for traders with limited capital.

Time Horizon: Debit spreads can have a longer time horizon, as they are not as dependent on time decay as credit spreads. You can choose expiration dates that align with your price forecast.

Implementing Credit Spreads:

To implement a credit spread:

Select a Strategy: Choose between a bear call spread or a bull put spread based on your market outlook.

Select Strike Prices: Determine the strike prices for the options that suit your strategy. Ensure the distance between strike prices aligns with your risk tolerance and profit potential.

Select Expiration Date: Choose an expiration date that matches your time horizon and trading goals.

Execute the Trade: Enter the trade by selling the short option and simultaneously buying the long option. This should result in net credit to your account.

Manage the Position: Continuously monitor the trade and consider closing it if you reach your profit target or if the market conditions change unfavorably.

Implementing Debit Spreads:

To implement a debit spread:

Select a Strategy: Choose between a bull call spread or a bear put spread based on your market outlook.

Select Strike Prices: Determine the strike prices for the options that suit your strategy. Ensure the distance between strike prices aligns with your risk tolerance and profit potential.

Select Expiration Date: Choose an expiration date that matches your time horizon and trading goals.

Execute the Trade: Enter the trade by buying the long option and simultaneously selling the short option. This should result in a net debit from your account.

Manage the Position: Continuously monitor the trade and consider closing it if you reach your profit target or if the market conditions change unfavorably.

In conclusion, credit spreads and debit spreads are versatile options trading strategies that cater to different market conditions and trader objectives. Credit spreads aim to generate income with limited risk, while debit spreads focus on risk management with defined costs. By understanding how these strategies work and when to use them, traders can build more effective and balanced options portfolios. However, it's important to remember that options trading carries inherent risks, and thorough research and risk management are essential for success in this arena.

Chapter 7

Vertical and Calendar Spreads

Vertical spreads and calendar spreads are popular options trading strategies that offer unique ways to profit from changes in price direction and the passage of time. While both strategies involve options, they serve different purposes and require distinct approaches. This comprehensive guide will delve into the intricacies of vertical and calendar spreads, providing you with a thorough understanding of how these strategies work, their differences, and when to use them.

Vertical Spreads: Profiting from Price Direction

Vertical spreads, also known as price spreads, are options strategies designed to profit from the price movement of an underlying asset. Traders use vertical spreads when they have a directional bias on the underlying security but want to reduce risk and cost compared to a simple long or short call or put option. Vertical spreads involve two options of the same type (either calls or puts) with different strike prices and the same expiration date. They can be classified into two main types: bull spreads and bear spreads.

Bull Vertical Spreads

Bull Call Spread: In this strategy, a trader simultaneously buys a lower strike call option and sells a higher strike call option with the same expiration date. It's used when the trader expects a moderate upward price movement in the underlying asset. The goal is to profit from the price increase while limiting potential losses.

Bull Put Spread: This strategy involves buying a higher strike put option and selling a lower strike put option with the same expiration date. It's employed when a trader anticipates a moderate increase in the underlying asset's price. The objective is to profit from the price rise while managing risk.

Bear Vertical Spreads

Bear Call Spread: In this approach, a trader buys a higher strike call option and sells a lower strike call option with the same expiration date. It's suitable when a trader believes the underlying asset's price will decrease moderately. The goal is to profit from the price drop while controlling potential losses.

Bear Put Spread: This strategy entails buying a lower strike put option and selling a higher strike put option with the same expiration date. It's used when a trader expects a moderate decline in the underlying asset's price. The aim is to profit from the price decrease while mitigating risk.

Profit Potential:

Vertical spreads offer limited profit potential, but they also limit potential losses. The profit is the difference between the strike prices minus the net premium paid or received. The maximum loss is capped at the initial premium paid to establish the spread.

Risk-Reward Profile:

These spreads have a defined risk-reward profile, making them suitable for traders with a specific price outlook on the underlying asset. They are often used to hedge existing positions or as income-generating strategies when combined with other options positions.

Calendar Spreads: Playing the Time Game

Calendar spreads, also known as time spreads or horizontal spreads, are options strategies that capitalize on the concept of time decay or theta. Unlike vertical spreads, calendar spreads involve options with the same strike price but different expiration dates. The primary goal of a calendar spread is to profit from the accelerated time decay of the short-term option relative to the longer-term option.

How Calendar Spreads Work:

To create a calendar spread, a trader simultaneously buys and sells options on the same underlying asset with the same strike price. However, the options have different expiration dates. Typically, the trader buys the longer-dated option (the one with a more extended expiration) and sells the shorter-dated option (the one with a nearer expiration). The options can be calls or puts, depending on the trader's outlook.

Profit Mechanism:

Calendar spreads profit when the underlying asset's price remains relatively stable, leading to the short-term option losing value at a faster rate than the longer-term option. The profit is the difference between the premium received from selling the near-term option and the premium paid for buying the longer-term option.

Risk-Reward Profile:

Calendar spreads offer a limited profit potential, which is the net premium received when establishing the spread. However, they also have limited risk, primarily the initial premium paid for the longer-term option. The risk-reward profile is advantageous when a trader expects minimal price movement in the underlying asset.

Understanding the Differences

Now that we have explored the fundamental concepts of vertical and calendar spreads let's delve into the key differences between these two options strategies:

Strategy Objective:

Vertical Spreads: These are primarily used to profit from the directional movement of an underlying asset. Traders use them when they have a specific price outlook.

Calendar Spreads: They aim to profit from time decay or theta. Traders use them when they expect the underlying asset to remain relatively stable in the short term.

Components:

Vertical Spreads: Involve options with different strike prices but the same expiration date.

Calendar Spreads: Involve options with the same strike price but different expiration dates.

Time Decay:

Vertical Spreads: Time decay can work for or against a vertical spread, depending on the specific strike prices chosen. It has a neutral impact if both options are at-the-money, while it can be positive or negative if one option is in-the-money and the other is out-of-the-money.

Calendar Spreads: Time decay is the primary driver of profit in calendar spreads. The short-term option loses value faster than the longer-term option, resulting in a profit.

Profit Potential:

Vertical Spreads: Offer limited profit potential, but losses are also capped. The profit or loss is determined by the difference in premiums between the options.

Calendar Spreads: Provide limited profit potential, usually derived from the premium received when selling the near-term option. Losses are also limited and typically involve the premium paid for the longer-term option.

Market Outlook:

Vertical Spreads: Require a specific directional bias in the market. They are used when a trader expects the underlying asset's price to move in a particular direction.

Calendar Spreads: Are used when a trader anticipates minimal price movement and seeks to profit from time decay.

Risk-Reward Profile:

Vertical Spreads: Offer a defined risk-reward profile, making them suitable for risk management and income generation strategies.

Calendar Spreads: Also provide a defined risk-reward profile, making them attractive for traders looking to benefit from time decay without taking on excessive risk.

When to Use Vertical Spreads or Calendar Spreads

The decision to use vertical spreads or calendar spreads depends on your market outlook, risk tolerance, and trading objectives. Here are some scenarios in which each strategy may be appropriate:

Vertical Spreads:

Strong Price Outlook: Use a vertical spread when you have a strong directional bias on an underlying asset and want to profit from that price movement.

Hedging: Employ vertical spreads to hedge an existing position, reducing downside risk while maintaining upside potential.

Income Generation: Combine vertical spreads with other options positions to generate income through premium collection.

Defined Risk: If you want to limit your potential losses and gains, vertical spreads are a suitable choice.

Calendar Spreads:

Neutral Outlook: Opt for a calendar spread when you expect the underlying asset to remain relatively stable in the short term and want to profit from time decay.

Time Decay Strategy: Use calendar spreads as part of a time decay strategy to capitalize on the accelerated erosion of the short-term option's value.

Low Volatility: Calendar spreads can be beneficial in low volatility markets where price movements are limited.

Limited Risk: If you prefer strategies with well-defined risk and reward parameters, calendar spreads offer this advantage.

Vertical spreads and calendar spreads are valuable tools in the options trader's toolkit. Understanding their differences and knowing when to use each strategy is crucial for successful trading. Vertical spreads allow you to profit from price direction while managing risk, while calendar spreads enable you to play the time decay game in a neutral or low volatility market.

Ultimately, the choice between vertical and calendar spreads should align with your market outlook, risk tolerance, and trading goals. By mastering both strategies, you can diversify your options trading approach and be better equipped to navigate various market conditions.

Chapter 8

Straddle and Strangle

Certainly! Let's delve deeper into the Straddle and Strangle options trading strategies, including their mechanics, advantages, and drawbacks.

Straddle Strategy: Profiting from Volatility

Mechanics:

A straddle is an options trading strategy where an investor simultaneously buys a call option and a put option with the same strike price and expiration date on the same underlying asset. This strategy is used to profit from significant price movements in either direction, irrespective of whether the asset's price goes up (bullish) or down (bearish).

Advantages:

Profit from Volatility: Straddles excel in highly volatile markets. They can be profitable when the market makes substantial moves, as the gain from one leg (call or put) compensates for the loss in the other leg.

Hedging: Straddles can also serve as a hedging strategy. Investors can use them to protect against unexpected price swings, providing insurance for their existing positions.

Predicting Breakouts: Straddles are often employed when traders expect a significant breakout but are uncertain about the direction. This strategy allows them to profit from a sharp move, regardless of whether it's upward or downward.

Drawbacks:

Costly: Buying both a call and a put option can be expensive, especially if the underlying asset is highly volatile. This cost can erode profits if the price doesn't move significantly.

Theta Decay: Time decay (theta) works against straddle holders. As time passes, the options lose value, which can lead to losses if the underlying asset's price remains relatively stable.

High Volatility Requirement: Straddles require substantial price movements to be profitable. In less volatile markets, the cost of the options may not be recouped.

Strangle Strategy: A Variation on the Theme

Mechanics:

A strangle is similar to a straddle but involves buying a call option and a put option with different strike prices while having the same expiration date on the same underlying asset. The call strike price is typically above the current asset price, and the put strike price is below it.

Advantages:

> Lower Cost: Strangles are generally cheaper than straddles because the options have different strike prices. This makes them more accessible for traders with limited capital.

> Profit from Volatility: Like straddles, strangles profit from significant price movements, making them suitable for volatile markets.

> Flexibility: Strangles offer more flexibility in predicting price direction than straddles since one of the options is usually out-of-the-money. This can reduce the initial cost and provide a wider profit range.

Drawbacks:

Still Costly: While strangles are cheaper than straddles, they can still be relatively expensive, especially in highly volatile markets.

Limited Profit Potential: The profit potential in strangles is capped because only one leg (call or put) will be in-the-money at expiration. This means that the strategy might not capture the full extent of a significant price move.

Time Decay: Like straddles, strangles are affected by time decay. If the asset price doesn't move significantly, both options can lose value.

In summary, both straddle and strangle strategies are designed to profit from volatility, but they have different cost structures and profit profiles. Traders should choose between them based on their market expectations, risk tolerance, and capital availability. These strategies can be effective when used judiciously but can also result in losses if market conditions don't align with the strategy's objectives.

Chapter 9

Iron Condor

An In-Depth Exploration of the Iron Condor Strategy

Introduction

The Iron Condor is a popular options trading strategy known for its ability to generate consistent income while managing risk. It's a versatile strategy that benefits from time decay and low volatility. In this comprehensive guide, we'll delve into the Iron Condor strategy, providing a step-by-step implementation guide, insights into risk management, and a discussion of its potential gains.

The Basics of Iron Condor

What is an Iron Condor?

An Iron Condor is an options trading strategy that involves the simultaneous sale of an out-of-the-money (OTM) call and an OTM put, combined with the purchase of a farther OTM call and put. This creates four-legged options spread that generates income through premium collection. The strategy is named "Iron Condor" due to the shape of its profit and loss (P&L) graph, which resembles the wings of a condor in flight.

Components of an Iron Condor

➢ Short Call: This is the first leg of the Iron Condor. You sell an OTM call option, typically with a strike price above the current market price of the underlying asset. This generates an upfront premium.

➢ Long Call: To limit potential losses on the short call, you buy a call option with a higher strike price, creating a bear call spread. This also requires an initial premium outlay.

➢ Short Put: The second leg of the Iron Condor involves selling an OTM put option, usually with a strike price below the current market price of the underlying asset. This generates another premium.

➢ Long Put: To protect against significant losses on the short put, you buy a put option with an even lower strike price, creating a bull put spread. Again, this leg requires an initial premium payment.

Objective of the Iron Condor

The primary objective of an Iron Condor is to profit from time decay and low volatility. As time passes and the underlying asset's price remains within a specified range (between the short call and short put strikes), the options you sold lose value, allowing you to buy them back at a lower cost or let them expire worthless. This difference between premium collection and premium expenditure represents your profit.

Step-by-Step Guide to Implementing the Iron Condor

Step 1: Select an Underlying Asset

Begin by selecting an underlying asset, such as a stock, ETF, or index, that you believe will trade within a defined range over the options' lifespan.

Step 2: Choose an Expiration Date

Select an expiration date for your options. Typically, traders choose options with a duration of 30 to 60 days, as this maximizes time decay.

Step 3: Determine the Strike Prices

Identify the strike prices for the short call and short put options. These should be above and below the current market price of the underlying asset, respectively. The distance between these strikes defines your "wing width."

Step 4: Execute the Trade

Execute the Iron Condor trade by simultaneously selling the short call and short put while buying the long call and long put. Ensure that the long call and long put strikes are farther from the short strikes, creating the defined risk range.

Step 5: Monitor and Manage

Continuously monitor your Iron Condor position, paying attention to changes in the underlying asset's price and volatility. You may need to make adjustments if the trade is threatened.

Risk Management and Potential Gains

Risk Management

- ❖ Max Loss: The maximum loss in an Iron Condor is limited to the difference between the strikes of the long call and short call (or long put and short put) minus the net premium received. To manage risk, it's essential to set stop-loss orders or take early action if the trade moves against you.

- ❖ Max Gain: The maximum gain is limited to the premium received when establishing the Iron Condor. To realize the maximum gain, the underlying asset should remain within the range defined by the short call and short put strikes at expiration.

- ❖ Delta and Gamma Risk: An Iron Condor is sensitive to changes in the underlying asset's price and volatility. Be aware of delta and gamma risks, which can impact your position. Adjustments, such as rolling the options or closing the position, may be necessary to mitigate these risks.

Potential Gains

- ❖ Consistent Income: Iron Condors are designed to generate income through premium collection. If the underlying asset trades within the defined range, you can profit from time decay as the options you sold lose value.

❖ Limited Risk: The risk in an Iron Condor is well-defined, making it suitable for risk-averse traders. You know your maximum potential loss upfront.

❖ Market Neutral: Iron Condors can be implemented in both bullish and bearish markets, making them versatile for various market conditions.

❖ High Probability: When structured correctly, Iron Condors have a high probability of success. This is because they profit as long as the underlying asset remains within the range you've chosen.

❖ Adjustment Opportunities: If the trade goes against you, there are adjustment strategies available, such as rolling the options or turning the Iron Condor into an Iron Butterfly, to mitigate losses.

Iron Condor is a powerful options trading strategy that offers the potential for consistent income while effectively managing risk. By following the steps outlined in this guide and implementing sound risk management practices, traders can harness the full potential of the Iron Condor strategy in their investment portfolios. However, it's crucial to remember that options trading involves inherent risks, and it's advisable to gain a thorough understanding of the strategy and practice it in a simulated environment before trading with real capital.

Chapter 10

Putting It All Together

Recap of Strategies Covered

In our journey through the exciting and often complex world of options trading, we've covered a wide range of strategies and techniques to help you build and manage a successful options portfolio. Options, as financial derivatives, offer traders the flexibility and potential for substantial profits while managing risk. As we recap the strategies covered, let's take a moment to reflect on the key takeaways from each:

- ❖ Covered Calls: We began with the covered call strategy, which involves holding a long position in an asset and selling a call option on that same asset. This strategy allows you to generate income from the premiums while potentially selling your assets at a higher price, but it caps your potential gains.

- ❖ Protective Puts: We then explored protective puts, a strategy that involves purchasing put options to hedge against potential downside risk in your portfolio. This strategy acts as insurance, allowing you to limit your losses if the market takes a downturn.

- ❖ Bullish Strategies: To capitalize on upward market movements, we delved into various bullish strategies, such as buying call options, vertical spreads, and ratio spreads. These strategies offer different risk-reward profiles, allowing you to fine-tune your approach based on your market outlook and risk tolerance.

❖ Bearish Strategies: Conversely, for bearish market expectations, we explored strategies like buying put options, bear put spreads, and ratio spreads. These strategies enable you to profit from declining asset prices while managing potential losses.

❖ Neutral Strategies: Recognizing that markets don't always move in a clear bullish or bearish direction, we covered neutral strategies like iron condors and iron butterflies. These strategies thrive in range-bound markets and can provide consistent returns when executed effectively.

❖ Income Strategies: Generating consistent income is a crucial objective for many options traders. We discussed strategies such as cash-secured puts, covered strangles, and credit spreads. These strategies aim to capitalize on time decay and market stability to generate regular premium income.

❖ Advanced Techniques: As we progressed, we introduced more advanced concepts like volatility trading, synthetic positions, and delta-neutral strategies. These techniques offer sophisticated ways to fine-tune your portfolio's risk and reward characteristics.

Tips for Managing Your Options Portfolio

Effective management of your options portfolio is paramount to long-term success. Here are some key tips to keep in mind:

❖ Diversification: Avoid putting all your eggs in one basket. Diversify your options positions across different asset classes, industries, and strategies to spread risk.

❖ Risk Management: Implement strict risk management rules. Determine the maximum percentage of your portfolio you're willing to risk on a single trade and stick to it.

❖ Continuous Learning: Options trading is dynamic and ever evolving. Stay up to date with market trends and new strategies by reading books, attending webinars, and following experienced traders.

❖ Portfolio Monitoring: Regularly review and adjust your portfolio as market conditions change. Keep an eye on open positions, adjust strike prices, and consider rolling options when necessary.

❖ Exit Strategies: Always have exit strategies in place before entering a trade. Decide your profit-taking and stop-loss levels to prevent emotional decision-making.

❖ Liquidity: Trade options with sufficient liquidity to ensure you can easily enter and exit positions at favorable prices.

Record Keeping: Maintain detailed records of your trades, including entry and exit prices, dates, and reasons for the trade. This helps in analyzing your performance and improving your strategies.

The Journey Ahead: Exploring Advanced Techniques

As you become more comfortable with options trading, you may be eager to explore advanced techniques that can elevate your portfolio management to the next level. Here are some avenues you can consider:

❖ Advanced Spread Strategies: Beyond basic vertical and horizontal spreads, explore advanced spread strategies like diagonal spreads, calendar spreads, and double diagonal spreads. These strategies involve different expiration dates and can be tailored to various market scenarios.

❖ Volatility Trading: Dive deeper into volatility trading by utilizing strategies like straddles and strangles. These thrive on price volatility and can be especially profitable during earnings announcements or major news events.

❖ Gamma Scalping: Learn about gamma scalping, a technique used by professional options traders to profit from short-term price movements and changes in option delta. This approach requires a deep understanding of the Greeks.

❖ Butterfly and Condor Adjustments: As you gain experience with iron butterflies and iron condors, explore techniques for adjusting these positions when the market moves against you. Adjustments can help salvage losing trades or turn them into winners.

❖ Portfolio Margin: Consider transitioning to a portfolio margin account if you meet the requirements. Portfolio margin can provide more leverage and reduced margin requirements, enabling you to manage a larger portfolio efficiently.

❖ Advanced Risk Management: Explore advanced risk management techniques such as tail risk hedging and position sizing based on portfolio volatility. These methods can help protect your capital in extreme market conditions.

❖ Algorithmic Trading: For those with programming skills, algorithmic options trading can be a rewarding avenue. Building custom trading algorithms allows you to automate your strategies and execute trades with precision.

❖ Options on Futures: If you're looking to diversify your portfolio, consider trading options on futures contracts. These offer exposure to commodities, interest rates, and various indices.

Conclusion

Options trading is a vast and dynamic field that offers a multitude of strategies and techniques for traders to explore. From the fundamental concepts of covered calls and protective puts to advanced tactics like gamma scalping and algorithmic trading, your options journey can be as simple or as sophisticated as you desire.

Overall, this comprehensive guide provides a solid foundation for understanding options trading, including strategies for different market conditions and risk tolerances. However, it's essential for investors to continue learning and practicing becoming proficient in options trading.

Remember that successful options trading requires continuous learning, disciplined risk management, and adaptability. As you put it all together and embark on the journey ahead, embrace the excitement and challenges of options trading, may your portfolio thrive in both bull and bear markets.

General Disclaimer:

The information provided in this book is for general informational purposes only. It should not be considered as professional financial, investment, or legal advice. The author is not a licensed financial advisor, and readers are encouraged to consult with qualified professionals before making any investment decisions.

Accuracy of Information:

The author has made reasonable efforts to ensure the accuracy of the information presented in this book at the time of writing. However, the financial and investment landscape is subject to change, and no guarantee is made regarding the accuracy, completeness, or timeliness of the content. Readers should verify any information before making investment decisions.

Investment Risks:

All investments carry inherent risks, and past performance is not indicative of future results. The author and publisher do not guarantee the success or profitability of any investment strategy or recommendation discussed in this book. Readers should conduct their own research and consider their individual financial circumstances before making investment decisions.

No Endorsement:

Any mention of specific investment products, services, or companies in this book should not be considered as an endorsement. The author and publisher do not endorse or recommend any particular investment products or services, and readers should exercise their own judgment when evaluating investment opportunities.

Legal Considerations:

Laws and regulations governing investments vary by jurisdiction. Readers are responsible for understanding and complying with the laws and regulations relevant to their location and financial situation. This book does not constitute legal advice.

Limitation of Liability:

The author and publisher shall not be held liable for any losses, damages, or legal actions arising from the use of the information provided in this book. Readers assume full responsibility for their investment decisions.

Changes to Disclaimer:

The author reserves the right to update or modify this disclaimer at any time without prior notice. It is the reader's responsibility to review the most current version of the disclaimer.

Consultation with Professionals:

Readers are strongly encouraged to seek the advice of qualified financial advisors, investment professionals, and legal experts before making any investment decisions or taking any financial actions based on the content of this book.